ESTHER
FROM START2FINISH

MICHAEL WHITWORTH

© 2025 by Start2Finish

All rights reserved. No part of this publication may be reproduced, stored in a retrieval system, or transmitted in any form or by any means without the prior written permission of the author. The only exception is brief quotations in printed reviews.

ISBN 978-1-944704-09-4

Published by Start2Finish
Bend, Oregon 97702
start2finish.org

Printed in the United States of America

Unless otherwise noted, all Scripture quotations are from The Holy Bible, English Standard Version®, copyright © 2001 by Crossway Bibles, a publishing ministry of Good News Publishers. Used by permission. All rights reserved.

Cover Design: Evangela Creative

CONTENTS

1. Pride on Display — 5
2. Providence in the Palace — 13
3. Pride's Plot Unleashed — 21
4. Courage for the Moment — 29
5. Pride Humbled, Faith Exalted — 37
6. Time to Speak — 45
7. Joy Remembered in Providence — 53

1

PRIDE ON DISPLAY

ESTHER 1

Objective: To see God's hidden providence amid human pride, folly, and power.

INTRODUCTION

Imagine walking through a grand parade of power—the kind where everything gleams and nothing lasts. Picture the bright lights of a political rally, a celebrity gala, or a corporate banquet where influence is measured by applause and wealth sparkles like armor. Such scenes dazzle the eyes but often hide deep insecurity beneath the surface. The book of Esther opens in a setting much like that—a royal spectacle meant to prove that one man ruled the world.

The book begins not with its heroine but with a king's party. The opening chapter is a display of power, wealth, and extravagance in the Persian capital of Susa. King Xerxes, ruler of the world's largest empire at the time, gathered nobles, officials, and citizens alike to witness his glory. For months he flaunted his riches and hosted a banquet unlike anything most had ever seen. Yet beneath the glittering gold and flowing wine lies a deeper truth: human power is fragile, and pride is destructive.

When Xerxes, drunk on wine and arrogance, summoned Queen Vashti to appear before his guests, she refused. Her "no" shocked the empire and exposed the king's insecurity. Advisors rushed to contain the fallout, turning one woman's defiance into a national crisis. The result was a decree that was both absurd and revealing: every man must be master in his own household. The irony is plain—the mightiest man alive couldn't control his own wife.

At first glance, Esther 1 looks like little more than palace drama. But for the reader, it is the opening move in a divine story. God's name is never mentioned, yet his providence fills the silence. The humiliation of a king and the dismissal of a queen prepare the way for Esther to rise and eventually for God's people to be saved. This chapter reminds us that even when life feels chaotic or meaningless, God is already working. What seems like disorder is often the very soil from which his purposes grow.

EXAMINATION

The king has a party (1:1-9)

The story of Esther opens not with Esther herself, but with a king, a queen, and a party that gets out of hand. It begins in the Persian citadel of Susa, where King Xerxes (or Ahasuerus, as he is called in Hebrew) reigned over a vast empire stretching from India to Ethiopia. From the first verse, the grandeur of the Persian kingdom is on full display. This was no ordinary kingdom; it was the superpower of its day, and Xerxes sat at the height of his glory. For six months he paraded his wealth and splendor before nobles, generals, and governors from across his empire. And when that was over, he held a seven-day feast for all the people in the citadel of Susa, from the greatest to the least.

The author paints a vivid picture of the palace. White and blue linen draped from marble pillars, couches made of silver and gold, pavements inlaid with mother-of-pearl and costly stones, golden goblets for wine, each one unique. This was not only luxury; it was propaganda. A Persian banquet was more than a dinner party. It was a political display of power, a reminder to all who attended that the wealth of the world flowed into the king's court and that he held control over it.

Wine flowed freely, and verse 8 tells us that "by the king's command each guest was allowed to drink in his own way." That may sound generous, but it was unusual. Normally, the drinking followed the king's example, and when he drank, everyone else drank. Here, he set no limits—every man could drink as much or as little as he wished. The scene is charged with indulgence, a perfect stage for what comes next.

Queen Vashti, meanwhile, hosted a banquet for the women of the palace. There's nothing unusual about this; Persian queens often acted independently and even owned estates, hosted gatherings, and managed their own resources. Vashti's banquet reminds us that though women in Persia were marginalized, they were not powerless.

The king's drunken command (1:10–15)

On the seventh day, when Xerxes was "in high spirits from wine," he gave a fateful order. He summoned Vashti to appear before the men wearing her royal crown so he could display her beauty to the guests. Here the glamour of the palace turns dark. We are not told exactly what Xerxes intended—whether he wished her to parade herself in some immodest fashion or simply to act as one more display item alongside his couches of gold and his goblets of wine. Either way, Vashti was treated not as a queen but as an object. And Vashti refused.

Her refusal set off a crisis. In a culture where the king's word was law, Vashti's "no" was staggering. Here is the most powerful man in the world, sitting on his throne, surrounded by nobles, drunk on his own glory—and his wife would not come. The text says, "The king became furious and burned with anger."

The counsel of the wise men (1:16–22)

Xerxes turned to his seven advisors, "men who understood the times," for counsel. What should be done to a queen who defies the king's command? One advisor, Memucan, escalated the matter. This was not merely a domestic dispute, he argued; Vashti's defiance threatened every household in the empire. "Every woman in the empire will hear of the queen's conduct," he claimed, "and there will be no end of disrespect and discord." What began as a personal embarrassment was suddenly an empire-wide crisis. Memucan urged Xerxes to depose Vashti and issue a royal decree that every man should be master in his own home.

The irony drips from the page. The most powerful man in the world couldn't manage his own household, so he issued an empire-wide law to save face. Persian decrees were considered irrevocable, yet the decree here was laughably hollow. You cannot legislate respect. If a man has to command honor, he's already lost it.

The satire is clear. The empire that claimed absolute control is shown to be petty and insecure. The king who ruled from India to Ethiopia can't get one woman to obey him. The advisors who claimed to protect the stability of the empire were driven by personal anxiety. The author of Esther is not so much concerned with gender politics as he is with exposing the weakness of worldly power.

And yet, this foolish decree had consequences. Vashti was removed, and a vacancy opened at the king's side. This is how the story of Esther begins to unfold. What looked like a palace scandal became the stage for God's hidden providence. Behind the pomp of Xerxes, behind the drunken banquets and insecure advisors, another hand was at work. In Esther there is a Power hidden from human eyes, manipulating events in ways that even the mightiest king can't resist.

This first chapter also sets the tone for the rest of the book. Again and again, we will see that the decrees of kings are not as final as they seem, that the power of the empire is a façade, and that the real Author of history is quietly steering events. Vashti's refusal is the first crack in the façade of Persian glory. Her courage—or perhaps her indignation—created a space in which Esther would later rise.

We should pause here and notice something important. The author of Esther does not evaluate Vashti's refusal. He doesn't call her rebellious, nor does he praise her as heroic. The text leaves her motives ambiguous. Was she acting nobly, refusing to be paraded before drunken men? Was she simply stubborn? We are not told. This silence is part of the author's design. Divine providence often works through human motives that are mixed, unclear, and ambiguous. God's hand is not limited to "ideal" circumstances; he works even in messy, compromised situations.

The chapter closes with Xerxes sending letters to every province in every language, declaring that every man should be ruler of his own household. Think of the irony: the largest postal service in the world mobilized, translators working overtime, decrees shipped to the corners of the empire—all to patch the king's wounded pride. The stage is set. Vashti is gone. And soon, the search will begin for a new queen.

APPLICATION

1. The fragility of pride

Xerxes ruled one of history's greatest empires, surrounded by wealth, luxury, and admiration. Yet a single act of defiance from Vashti shattered his composure. Pride often appears strong, but it is as fragile as glass. It depends on others' recognition and quickly crumbles when respect is withheld. Scripture warns, "Pride goes before destruction, and a haughty spirit before a fall" (Prov. 16:18). Xerxes' humiliation began not in battle but in his own palace. The same happens to us when pride rules our hearts. We become brittle, easily offended, and obsessed with control. Pride isolates us from others and blinds us to correction. The gospel calls us instead to humility—the strength that bows before God and serves others. Lasting honor comes not from asserting ourselves, but from surrendering our pride to the One who lifts up the humble.

2. The folly of indulgence

The writer of Esther makes a subtle but important observation: Xerxes gave his command "when his heart was merry with wine." The king's judgment was clouded by indulgence, and one rash decision altered the course of an empire. Sin often begins in such moments—when desire dulls discernment. Indulgence may promise freedom, but it enslaves the will. Whether through drunkenness, pleasure, or unchecked appetite, our hearts are easily led astray. Scripture contrasts this loss of control with Paul's charge: "Do not get drunk with wine... but be filled with the Spirit" (Eph. 5:18). The issue is control—what fills and directs our hearts. When we live under the Spirit's influence, wisdom governs desire, and grace tempers impulse. Xerxes teaches us that indulgence leads to folly, but discipline guided by God's Spirit leads to peace, self-control, and lasting joy.

3. The limits of forced respect

When Vashti defied the king, Xerxes and his counselors issued decrees to ensure that "every man should be master in his own house." They sought respect through legislation rather than character. Yet true honor cannot be demanded—it must be earned. Those who insist on obedience through fear reveal weakness, not strength. The greatest leaders in Scripture modeled humility and service. Jesus washed the feet of his disciples to show that in God's kingdom, authority flows downward in love. Husbands, fathers, elders, and rulers alike must learn this pattern: influence grows through service, not coercion. Forced respect breeds resentment; servant leadership wins hearts. Xerxes' command failed because it lacked moral weight. In our homes, churches, and communities, let us lead as Jesus led—by giving rather than grasping, serving rather than shouting, and earning trust through Christlike character.

4. The providence within the mess

Esther 1 offers no heroes, only flawed people colliding in pride and conflict. Yet through their failures, God's unseen plan begins to unfold. Vashti's removal paved the way for Esther's rise and ultimately for Israel's deliverance. Providence often looks messy in the moment—like threads tangled beyond repair—but in hindsight we see God weaving redemption through chaos. The same truth comforts us when our own lives unravel. God's control does not depend on human virtue. He works through sinners, mistakes, and even injustice to accomplish his purpose. What seems like random disorder is the stage on which divine order is revealed. If God could use a drunken king and a humiliated queen to protect his people, he can use our imperfect stories too. Providence assures us that nothing is wasted when God holds the pen.

5. The faith to trust God's silence

God's name never appears, yet his presence fills every shadowed corner of the story. He does not speak, but he acts. He does not appear, but he directs. This silence can feel unsettling, especially when prideful powers seem to rule the day. Yet faith often begins where visibility ends. Psalm 121:4 reminds us that God "neither slumbers nor sleeps." Even when we cannot trace his hand, we can trust his heart. Seasons of silence test and strengthen our faith, teaching us to wait, pray, and believe that God's purposes advance unseen. Xerxes may have ruled the empire, but God ruled history. The same is true today. When heaven seems quiet, believers must rest in the assurance that divine providence is still writing the story—and the ending belongs to him alone.

CONCLUSION

Esther 1 is more than a royal scandal—it is a mirror reflecting the frailty of human pride and the quiet strength of God's providence. Xerxes strutted in wealth yet crumbled at rejection. His advisors masked fear with decrees that only revealed their insecurity. In contrast, the God who is never named in this chapter is already shaping events for his glory. We learn that pride leads to downfall, indulgence clouds judgment, and forced respect is empty. Above all, we see that God works through the broken, the messy, and the ordinary to accomplish his plans. What looks chaotic to us is never outside his control.

REFLECTION

1. What does the royal banquet reveal about Xerxes' power and priorities?
2. Why was Vashti's refusal so shocking and significant in Persian culture?
3. How did Memucan interpret Vashti's defiance, and what remedy did he suggest?
4. How does this story expose the irony and weakness of Persian power?
5. How is God's providence shown, even though his name is never mentioned?
6. How does irony reveal the foolishness behind Xerxes' household decree?

DISCUSSION

1. How does pride today make people fragile instead of strong?
2. What modern indulgences cloud judgment and lead to unwise choices?
3. How do we sometimes try to control respect rather than earn it?
4. How does God work through messy or uncertain situations in your life?
5. How can we trust God's providence when he seems silent or hidden?
6. How can we practice servant leadership daily in our families, workplaces, and churches?

2

PROVIDENCE IN THE PALACE
ESTHER 2:1-18

Objective: To trust God's providence when His hand seems hidden.

INTRODUCTION

Sometimes the most important stories begin with what seems ordinary—or even foolish. Think of the way a chess game unfolds: the early moves look small and insignificant, but each one quietly shapes the outcome. A single pawn advanced, a piece moved into place—none seem decisive at first, yet together they set the stage for victory. In much the same way, the book of Esther shows how God works through ordinary moments and imperfect people to accomplish extraordinary purposes. What looks like coincidence is often providence in disguise.

When we left chapter 1, the mighty King Xerxes had been humbled by the refusal of Queen Vashti. His ego bruised, he deposed her and issued decrees to save face. But time passed. The king marched against Greece, suffered crushing defeats, and returned home with his pride wounded once more. The man who once displayed wealth for months on end was now desperate for comfort. His attendants suggested an empire-wide search for a new queen, gathering young women from every province. What seems like a shallow attempt to soothe his insecurity would become the stage for God's providence.

Into this story step Mordecai and Esther, Jews living in exile. Mordecai had raised his orphaned cousin, and through a series of events beyond her control, Esther was swept into the royal harem. She rose quickly, winning favor with everyone who met her, and eventually with the king himself. In time, she was crowned queen of Persia. To the world, this looked like chance or beauty. To the eyes of faith, it was God at work—quietly, invisibly, preparing his servant for the salvation of his people.

EXAMINATION

The plan for a new queen (2:1–4)

The scandal of Vashti's refusal and banishment left the Persian court shaken. What began as a display of power in chapter 1 ended in humiliation for King Xerxes, the most powerful man in the world who could not control his own household. Chapter 2 opens after some time has passed—nearly four years, in fact. In that period Xerxes had marched against Greece, suffered crushing defeats, and returned to Persia a shadow of the proud ruler who had once paraded his wealth for months on end. The king who had strutted in glory now sat deflated, nursing his shame and looking for comfort. This is the moment when his attendants proposed a solution: let a new queen be found.

The search for a queen (2:5–11)

The plan was simple in concept but massive in scope. From every province of the empire, young women of beauty were to be gathered into the royal harem. They would undergo twelve months of cosmetic treatments and then be presented one by one to the king, who would choose the one that pleased him most.

To modern ears the arrangement sounds cruel, and it was. These women were taken from their families, paraded before the king, and if they did not win his favor, they were consigned to the harem as concubines, never to return home. This was not a fairy-tale romance or a royal love story; it was an act of control, a king's attempt to soothe his ego with beauty and pleasure. Yet even here, in this distorted and demeaning system, God was at work.

At this point the story introduces Mordecai, a Jew from the tribe of Benjamin, descended from the exiles carried away by Nebuchadnezzar.

He lived in the citadel of Susa and had raised his cousin Hadassah, also known by her Persian name, Esther. Already the tension of identity is felt. Hadassah—"myrtle" in Hebrew—spoke of her Jewish roots, but Esther—possibly from the Persian word for "star"—was the name she bore in her adopted culture. She was an orphan raised in exile, caught between two worlds. Yet this ordinary young woman, with no royal lineage, no great wealth, and no claim to power, would be thrust into the very heart of Persian politics.

The text notes that Esther was lovely in form and features, and her beauty drew the attention of the king's officials. She was taken into the harem, where she quickly won the favor of Hegai, the eunuch in charge. He provided her with the best food, attendants, and living quarters. It is here that we begin to see a theme that will recur throughout the book: Esther "found favor." At every turn, those who met her looked upon her with kindness and admiration. The narrator does not make a show of it, but behind that favor lay the unseen providence of God. What looked like mere coincidence—the right glance at the right time, the right words spoken to the right person—was in fact God weaving his purposes quietly into place.

Mordecai, though left outside the palace gates, remained deeply concerned for Esther. Day by day he walked near the courtyard to check on her and learn how she was doing. Here we see a sharp contrast. The king, though surrounded by wealth, was consumed by his own appetite and pride. Mordecai, with no throne and no power, showed genuine love and vigilance. In his concern for his cousin, we glimpse something of the covenant faithfulness of God himself, who watches over his people even when they are exiles in a foreign land.

One striking detail in the story is Esther's silence about her Jewish identity. Mordecai had instructed her not to reveal it, and she obeyed. Why such secrecy? Perhaps Mordecai feared prejudice against Jews, or perhaps he recognized that the time was not right for her heritage to be known. Whatever the reason, Esther kept her identity hidden, a choice that would become central to the unfolding drama. The tension of living as God's people in exile runs throughout the book: to what extent should they assimilate, and when must they stand apart? Esther's silence at this stage is not cowardice but wisdom. There is a time to speak and a time to be silent, and the moment for her voice had not yet come.

The women's preparation and the king's choice (2:12-17)

The description of the women's preparation is both lavish and heartbreaking. For twelve months, they were given oils and perfumes, cosmetics and treatments, as though their entire worth could be distilled to the surface of their appearance. Then, when their turn came, they spent one night with the king. If he delighted in them, they might rise to prominence. If not, they were dismissed to a life of lonely luxury, bound forever to the harem with no hope of marriage or children outside its walls. It is a sobering reminder of the emptiness of worldly systems that promise glory but deliver captivity.

When Esther's turn arrived, she distinguished herself by asking for nothing more than what Hegai, the eunuch, advised. In other words, she trusted his wisdom rather than demanding her own preferences. This humility set her apart from the others, and once again, "she won the favor of everyone who saw her." The king himself was taken with her. The text says that Xerxes loved Esther more than all the other women, and she found more favor and approval with him than any of the others. In the tenth month of the seventh year of his reign (December 479 or January 478 BC), he placed the royal crown upon her head and declared her queen in Vashti's place.

Esther's coronation banquet (2:18)

True to his nature, Xerxes marked the occasion with another feast. He called it Esther's banquet, declared a holiday throughout the provinces, and distributed gifts with royal liberality. In the first chapter, the king's banquet ended in disgrace, his pride wounded by Vashti's refusal. Now, years later, another banquet celebrated the rise of a Jewish orphan to the throne of Persia. What the empire meant for indulgence and control, God was using to prepare deliverance.

APPLICATION

1. God works through imperfect circumstances

Esther 2 reminds us that God's providence operates through situations that are neither ideal nor chosen. Esther did not volunteer to join the king's harem. Mordecai never intended for his cousin to rise in a foreign palace. Yet through these unplanned events, God quietly advanced his redemptive purpose. We often expect his will to unfold in straight lines and shining clarity, but his guidance usually weaves through confusion, disappointment, and delay. The comfort of this passage lies in knowing that God is not frustrated by the messiness of life. He redeems it. Every twist of our story, even the painful ones, can serve his greater plan. When life feels out of control, this chapter reminds us that providence thrives in imperfection and that no circumstance lies beyond God's transforming reach.

2. True power belongs to God alone

This chapter dismantles our illusions about power and control. Xerxes appeared unstoppable—commanding armies, wealth, and women—but his strength proved shallow. His great "search" for a queen was only an attempt to comfort his bruised pride. In contrast, a powerless orphan named Esther was being quietly positioned by God to change the fate of nations. Worldly influence, beauty, and wealth may dazzle for a season, but real power belongs to God alone. Human rulers strut and posture, but their authority is temporary and derivative. Every empire stands on borrowed breath. Believers can take heart in this truth when governments fail, leaders disappoint, or systems seem corrupt. God's sovereignty never falters. His purposes advance unhindered beneath the surface of human ambition. The One who ruled in Susa still rules today, working through the weak to humble the proud.

3. Living faithfully in a compromised world

Esther carried two names—Hadassah and Esther—and lived in two worlds, Jewish and Persian. Her silence about her identity was not cowardice but discernment. She teaches us that faithfulness in exile requires wisdom. There is a time to speak boldly and a time to stay silent, a time to blend in and a time to stand apart. God's people must navigate a culture that rarely shares their convictions, and that task demands grace as much as courage. Esther's example reminds us that even when our choices feel ambiguous, God's hand is not absent. He can use imperfect people who live in tension between faith and culture. Like Esther, we are called to live faithfully in the world without belonging to it—trusting that God's purpose is unfolding even when our situation seems morally complex or spiritually unclear.

4. Trusting the hidden hand of providence

Though God's name never appears in Esther 2, his presence fills every detail. He gave Esther favor with Hegai, wisdom in her humility, and grace in the eyes of the king. The silence of heaven is not the silence of absence but of unseen activity. We too live in seasons when God seems quiet—when prayer feels unanswered and chaos fills the headlines. Yet this passage assures us that divine providence never sleeps. God works in the shadows as surely as he does in the spotlight. Faith, then, means trusting the Author even when we cannot see the script. The task of God's people is not to predict his plan but to rest in his presence. In exile or obscurity, in fear or uncertainty, we can trust that the same God who guided Esther still guides his people today.

CONCLUSION

Esther 2 shows us that God's providence often unfolds in ways we least expect. A young Jewish orphan, swept into a pagan king's harem, rose to the throne of Persia—not by her own power, but by the hidden hand of God. The world saw only beauty, politics, and chance, but faith sees providence preparing salvation. Esther's story reminds us that our lives, too, are never outside God's care. He is present in the quiet, working through details we may overlook, arranging the future even in moments that feel uncertain. The chapter invites us to trust him, knowing that no circumstance is beyond his redeeming purpose.

REFLECTION

1. How much time passed between Vashti's removal and Esther's selection as queen?
2. What plan did Xerxes' attendants suggest to find a new queen?
3. Who were Mordecai and Esther, and what was their family background?
4. Why did Esther hide her Jewish identity, and whose advice did she follow?
5. How did Esther earn favor in the harem and stand out from others?
6. What events led to Esther's coronation, and how did Xerxes celebrate her rise?

DISCUSSION

1. How can Christians live "in the world" without becoming shaped by it?
2. How can we know when to speak up and when to stay silent?
3. What does Xerxes' insecurity reveal about the weakness of worldly power today?
4. How might God use our ordinary qualities to accomplish his purposes?
5. When have you recognized God's hand in painful or unexpected circumstances?
6. How can we trust God's hidden work when his presence feels silent?

3

PRIDE'S PLOT UNLEASHED

ESTHER 2:19–3:15

Objective: To trust God's providence
when pride and hostility seem to rule.

INTRODUCTION

History—and our own lives—are often shaped not by grand decisions, but by small moments that seem insignificant at the time. A word spoken in anger, an overlooked kindness, a promotion undeserved—all can set in motion events far beyond what anyone intended. Think of how a spark in dry grass can become a wildfire. What begins as something small soon consumes everything in its path.

The story of Esther turns sharply in this section. Up to this point, the narrative has been marked by feasts, beauty contests, and court intrigue. But now the stakes rise dramatically. Mordecai's quiet loyalty in exposing a plot against the king went unrewarded, while a new character, Haman the Agagite, rose to power. Haman's wounded pride at Mordecai's refusal to bow festered into hatred, and hatred hardened into a plan for genocide. The empire's couriers galloped across the provinces carrying decrees of death, and the Jewish people were plunged into danger and despair.

What is striking is how ordinary the path to catastrophe seems. A forgotten good deed, a prideful man promoted, a careless king manipulated by flattery—these are the threads that form a crisis. Yet behind it all, God's unseen hand was still at work. The lot may have been cast, but the outcome belonged to him. The couriers may have carried orders of destruction, but another story was unfolding. In this tension between human pride and divine providence, the book of Esther teaches us how to live faithfully when the world seems hostile and God seems silent.

EXAMINATION

Mordecai uncovers a plot (2:19-23)

The end of Esther 2 sets up a dramatic shift. Mordecai, who had been faithfully watching over Esther from the palace gates, uncovered a plot by two of the king's officials to assassinate Xerxes. He relayed the information through Esther, who reported it in his name, and the plot was stopped. The conspirators were executed, and the matter recorded in the royal chronicles. It is striking, however, that no honor or reward was given to Mordecai at this time. The omission was not accidental; it is a detail the author will later use with great irony when the king's sleepless night in chapter 6 changes the entire story. For now, Mordecai's loyalty went unrecognized, even as others in the court were being promoted.

The rise of Haman (3:1-5)

When chapter 3 opens, we are introduced to Haman. His name and title mark him as an outsider—an Agagite, tied symbolically to Israel's ancient enemy, the Amalekites. The mention of Agag immediately recalls the story of Saul, Israel's first king, who failed to obey God fully in defeating the Amalekites and sparing their king (1 Sam. 15). Mordecai, a descendant of Saul's tribe, and Haman, an Agagite, are set in deliberate opposition. Their conflict is not only personal but also a continuation of an ancient struggle between God's people and their enemies.

Xerxes promoted Haman above all the other officials, granting him a seat of honor. The king commanded that all his servants bow before Haman, showing him reverence. But Mordecai refused. The text gives no lengthy explanation—only that he would not bow down or pay him homage. Some suggest Mordecai objected because of Haman's Agagite lineage; others argue that it was because such honor crossed a line reserved for

God alone. Whatever the reason, Mordecai's refusal set him on a collision course with Haman.

Day after day the king's servants questioned Mordecai, and day after day he stood firm. At last they reported him to Haman, who was enraged. To Haman, Mordecai's defiance was not simply personal insult—it became the seed of genocidal hatred. When he learned Mordecai was a Jew, Haman resolved not merely to punish him, but to destroy all Jews throughout the empire.

Haman's hatred and the casting of lots (3:6–7)

The escalation is staggering. One man's refusal leads to an entire people marked for death. But the book of Esther shows this is how pride and power operate. Just as Xerxes' wounded pride in chapter 1 led to decrees affecting every woman in the empire, so Haman's wounded pride now threatened every Jew. The author wants us to see the absurdity of it. Worldly power is insecure, unstable, and often reckless. A fragile ego can unleash horrors across nations.

Haman cast the *pur*—that is, the lot—to determine the day for this destruction. He trusted chance and superstition to guide his hand, but Proverbs reminds us, "The lot is cast into the lap, but its every decision is from the Lord" (16:33). Even as Haman schemed, the unseen hand of God was setting the timetable for deliverance.

Haman's deceit and the king's carelessness (3:8–15)

When Haman presented his case to Xerxes, he did so with cunning half-truths. He described the Jews as a people scattered yet distinct, whose laws were different and who did not obey the king's commands. He concluded they were a danger to the empire and should be destroyed. To sweeten the deal, he offered the king an enormous sum of silver for the royal treasury, essentially bribing him for the decree. Xerxes, careless as ever, handed over his signet ring and said, "Keep the money and do with the people as you please." The most powerful man in the world signed away the lives of an entire people without a thought.

The decree went out, sealed with the king's authority and sent to every province in every language. On the thirteenth day of the twelfth month (March 7, 473 BC), all Jews—young and old, men and women—were to be annihilated and their goods plundered. The machinery of empire was mobilized for genocide. And as the couriers sped out with the message, the king and Haman sat down to drink, while the city of Susa was bewildered. The contrast is chilling: the rulers indulged themselves in luxury while their subjects reeled at the horror of their decree.

Several themes emerge here. First, we see again the incompetence of Xerxes. He appears in these chapters as little more than a rubber stamp for the schemes of his advisors. Whether manipulated by Memucan in chapter 1, by his attendants in chapter 2, or now by Haman in chapter 3, the king's "absolute power" is shown to be hollow. His empire moves at the whim of others.

Second, the story underscores the destructive power of pride. Haman's rage at one man becomes hatred toward an entire people. Pride magnifies slights, turns wounds into vendettas, and poisons hearts until they lash out with devastating force.

Third, Esther 2:19–3:15 illustrates the recurring biblical theme that God's people will face threats in this world. From Pharaoh's decree against Hebrew boys, to Nebuchadnezzar's furnace, to Darius' lions' den, the people of God often live at the mercy of hostile powers. Yet the deeper truth is that those powers never have the final word. Though God's name is not mentioned, his providence frames the entire narrative. Mordecai's unrewarded loyalty will resurface at exactly the right time. Haman's lot-casting will set the stage for God's deliverance. The reckless decree of the king will only magnify the triumph of God's hand.

Finally, the text draws our eyes forward to Esther. She has not yet spoken, but the stage is being set for her voice to emerge. Mordecai has shown courage in standing firm. Haman has revealed his venom. The king has revealed his folly. And now the queen, silent until this point, will soon be called upon to decide whether she will risk her life to save her people.

In these verses, the conflict is drawn in bold lines: pride against humility, hatred against faithfulness, chance against providence. The forces of darkness seem ascendant, but the story whispers that God is already preparing salvation. The couriers may carry decrees of death, but another Word rules history, unseen yet unstoppable. The throne of Persia is not ultimate. The God of Israel still reigns.

APPLICATION

1. The destructive power of pride

This section of Esther exposes how pride corrodes the soul and destroys community. Haman's fury began with one man's refusal to bow but erupted into genocidal hatred. Pride magnifies small slights into major offenses and demands that everyone cater to our ego. Scripture warns that "pride goes before destruction" (Prov. 16:18), and Haman's example shows why. When pride rules the heart, relationships shatter, and compassion withers. We may not plot harm as he did, but pride still wreaks havoc—in marriages, friendships, and churches. It insists on control, resists correction, and refuses forgiveness. Pride blinds us to truth and drives us to defend our image rather than our integrity. Esther reminds us that humility is strength. The antidote to pride is surrender—choosing to serve others, to yield before God, and to let his glory, not ours, define success.

2. The emptiness of worldly power

Xerxes ruled the largest empire on earth, yet his throne was hollow. He was easily swayed by others and signed away countless lives without thought or remorse. His "absolute power" was nothing more than a façade built on fear and vanity. The same illusion persists today. Political might, corporate wealth, and social influence may appear unstoppable, but they are fragile before the sovereignty of God. Scripture repeatedly reminds us not to fear earthly rulers but to revere the Lord who reigns above them all. Xerxes' weakness warns us not to mistake position for authority or appearance for substance. The Christian's security does not rest in governments, leaders, or systems, but in the unshakable reign of Christ. When earthly powers seem dominant, God's people must stand firm, knowing that every empire will crumble—but his kingdom endures forever.

3. The cost of faithful conviction

Mordecai's refusal to bow to Haman was not arrogance but conviction. He would not compromise his allegiance to God, even at the cost of safety. His courage reminds us that faithfulness often provokes hostility. Jesus told his followers, "If the world hates you, know that it has hated me before it hated you" (John 15:18). Believers should not be shocked when obedience invites opposition. The measure of faith is not whether we escape hardship but whether we remain steadfast under pressure. Like Mordecai, we are called to quiet courage—a resolve to honor God when compromise seems easier. Hostility may expose us, isolate us, or cost us dearly, but it also proves that our loyalty lies with heaven, not the world. The faithful heart rests in this assurance: persecution may test us, but it cannot defeat what God sustains.

4. The certainty of God's hidden providence

Esther 2:19–3:15 reminds us that God's providence is never absent, even when invisible. Mordecai's unrewarded loyalty, Haman's casting of lots, and the king's reckless decree all seemed random or unjust—but each event served a greater purpose. God's sovereignty ruled over every coincidence, turning chaos into opportunity for deliverance. Likewise, our lives may seem governed by unfair people, bad timing, or meaningless suffering. Yet the story of Esther assures us that nothing escapes God's control. The hands of prideful men never outweigh the will of a faithful God. His plans may unfold slowly, but they never fail. Faith means trusting that his unseen work is sure, even when his presence feels distant. The God who governed Persia's palace still governs our paths. In every hidden moment, he prepares redemption, proving that providence may be silent—but it is never still.

CONCLUSION

Esther 2:19–3:15 sets the stage for one of Scripture's great reversals. Mordecai's loyalty went unnoticed, Haman's pride exploded into hatred, and Xerxes' carelessness endangered an entire people. Yet even in these dark moments, God's providence was quietly at work. The story reminds us that pride is destructive, power is fragile, and hostility toward God's people is real—but above all, it assures us that God's purposes cannot be thwarted. When life feels ruled by chance, pride, or reckless decisions, Esther teaches us to look deeper. The unseen God is writing a story of deliverance that will not fail.

REFLECTION

1. What plot did Mordecai uncover, and how was it reported and resolved?
2. Who was Haman, and why is being an Agagite important?
3. Why did Mordecai refuse to bow before Haman?
4. How did Haman's pride turn insult into a plan for genocide?
5. What purpose did casting the *pur* serve in Haman's plot?
6. How did Xerxes react to Haman's request, and what followed for the Jews?

DISCUSSION

1. How can we guard against pride that turns small offenses into resentment?
2. How do today's leaders resemble Xerxes in being easily influenced by others?
3. How can we prepare to face hostility for remaining faithful to God?
4. How does this story inspire trust when life feels ruled by chance?
5. What unrewarded details in your life might God use for future good?
6. How does trusting God's hidden providence strengthen courage against powerful opposition?

4

COURAGE FOR THE MOMENT
ESTHER 4:1-5:8

Objective: To embrace courage and trust God's providence in critical moments.

INTRODUCTION

Moments of decision often come without warning. A soldier steps forward while others shrink back. A firefighter runs into a burning building. A friend speaks up when silence would be safer. Courage is rarely convenient—it arrives when the cost is highest.

The tension in Esther reaches its breaking point in chapters 4–5. Haman's decree of destruction had spread through the empire, and the Jewish people were thrown into mourning. Sackcloth and ashes replaced banquets and laughter. Mordecai grieved openly at the king's gate, while Esther remained isolated in the palace, removed from the suffering of her people. The gap between her position and her heritage could not have been wider.

Through a messenger, Mordecai urged her to intercede with the king. Esther hesitated, knowing the risk: to enter the throne room uninvited was to court death. Yet Mordecai's words struck deeply: "Who knows but that you have come to the kingdom for such a time as this?" Suddenly the moment of decision arrived. Would Esther remain silent and safe, or would she risk her life for her people?

EXAMINATION

Mourning in Susa (4:1–5)

Up to this point, the narrative has mingled banquets, beauty, and court intrigue. But when the decree for annihilation spread through the empire, laughter and wine gave way to sackcloth and ashes. The frivolity of the palace is replaced by the lament of God's people. The Jews mourned publicly, fasting, weeping, and crying out in anguish. At the center of their grief stood Mordecai, who tore his clothes, covered himself with ashes, and stationed himself at the king's gate, unable to enter because of his mourning attire. What began as a personal feud between Haman and Mordecai now threatened the survival of an entire people.

News of Mordecai's public grief soon reached Esther. But she remained insulated within the palace, separated from her people's suffering. At first, she did not know why her cousin mourned so bitterly. She sent him clothes to replace his sackcloth, as though the problem could be solved by changing garments. This moment shows how removed she had become from the life of her people. As queen, she lived in luxury but was sheltered from the despair that gripped her nation.

Mordecai's plea to Esther (4:6–14)

Through the intermediary Hathach, Mordecai explained the situation. He even told Esther of the money Haman had promised to contribute to the royal treasury in exchange for Jewish lives. He urged Esther to intercede with the king. His words were not merely a suggestion but a command, spoken with the authority of the guardian who had raised her from childhood. Esther's first response was hesitation. She reminded Mordecai that anyone who approached the king unsummoned risked immediate execution unless the king extended his golden scepter. And she confessed she had not been summoned for thirty days.

Her reluctance is understandable. She faced a genuine dilemma: risk her life to speak or remain silent and preserve her safety. But Mordecai's reply cut through her fear. He reminded her that silence would not guarantee survival. "Do not think you alone will escape," he warned. "If you keep quiet, deliverance for the Jews will come from elsewhere—but you and your family will perish. And who knows but that you have come to royal position for such a time as this?"

These words frame the theology of Esther. Though God's name is never mentioned, his providence is assumed. Mordecai's conviction is clear: deliverance will come. The only question is whether Esther will embrace her role in God's plan or shrink back. His words press her—and us—into the tension between God's sovereignty and human responsibility. God will accomplish his purposes, but his people are called to courage, to faith, and to action.

Esther's resolve and the call to fast (4:15–17)

Esther's response marks her transformation. No longer passive, no longer silent, she took command of the situation. She instructed Mordecai to gather all the Jews in Susa to fast for three days on her behalf, while she and her attendants did the same. Then, resolved, she declared: "I will go to the king, even though it is against the law. And if I perish, I perish." These are the words of a woman who had embraced her calling, even at the cost of her life. For the first time, Esther spoke with authority and conviction, stepping into the role God had prepared for her.

The invitation to a banquet (5:1–8)

Chapter 5 records the fulfillment of her resolution. On the third day, after fasting, Esther put on her royal robes and stood in the inner court of the palace. The suspense is palpable. Would Xerxes extend the golden scepter or order her death? The narrator slows the action, describing the scene in detail: the king on his throne, Esther in the court, the risk of death hanging over her. At last, Xerxes saw her, was pleased with her, and extended the scepter. She approached, touched the tip, and lived.

The king, in a burst of generosity, offered Esther whatever she wished, up to half the kingdom. This was a royal idiom, not meant literally, but it underscores the favor Esther had won. Instead of making her petition immediately, Esther invited the king and Haman to a banquet. There, once again, the king repeated his extravagant offer, but Esther delayed once more, inviting them to another banquet the next day. Was she fearful, or was she strategic? Many suggest her delay was deliberate. By waiting, she heightened the king's curiosity, ensured Haman's presence, and prepared the stage for the reversal that was to come.

The effect was masterful. Esther, once the silent and passive girl swept into the harem, was now the one directing the course of events. She dictated the timing, set the stage, and moved the story forward. Her courage, rooted in fasting and prayer, was matched by her wisdom in waiting for the right moment.

This passage teaches us that courage is not the absence of fear but the resolve to act despite fear. Esther's words, "If I perish, I perish," echo the faith of Shadrach, Meshach, and Abednego before the fiery furnace, and the words of Jesus in Gethsemane, "Not my will but yours be done." It is the language of surrender—entrusting one's life fully to God.

At the same time, Esther models patience and discernment. She does not rush recklessly but acts with prudence. Courage and wisdom together form the path of faithful obedience. And behind her every move is the unseen hand of God, guiding his servant to the moment when she will speak the words that change history.

By the end of this section, the crisis has not yet been resolved, but the tide has begun to turn. Mordecai has called Esther to her defining moment, and Esther has embraced it. The people have fasted, the queen has resolved, and the king has extended his scepter. Haman, unsuspecting, enjoys the honor of a royal banquet, even as the trap begins to close around him. The stage is set for God's deliverance.

APPLICATION

1. When fear collides with faith

This section of Esther forces us to ask how we respond when fear challenges faith. Esther faced a choice: remain silent and safe, or speak up and risk everything. Her dilemma mirrors our own moments of moral or spiritual testing. Will we stand for Christ when it costs us comfort, reputation, or security? True faith does not erase fear—it redefines it. Faith moves forward even when the outcome is uncertain. Courage is not the absence of trembling, but obedience in spite of it. Esther teaches us that silence may offer temporary safety, but it forfeits eternal significance. God's people are called to act, not because they are fearless, but because they trust the One who rules over fear itself. When faith and fear collide, the faithful heart steps forward, believing that obedience is always safer than compromise.

2. Providence and purpose in every place

Mordecai's words to Esther reveal a deep confidence in God's providence.

He believed deliverance would come—if not through Esther, then through someone else. God's plans cannot fail. Yet Mordecai also challenged her to recognize that she might have been placed in her royal position "for such a time as this." That statement captures one of Scripture's greatest truths: none of us is where we are by accident. Our families, workplaces, and opportunities are arranged by God's design. We often see randomness, but he sees purpose. The challenge is to trust that our current circumstances, however ordinary or difficult, fit within his redemptive plan. Like Esther, we must be ready when the moment of faithfulness comes. God's providence gives meaning to our placement; our responsibility is to respond with faith, courage, and readiness when he calls.

3. The power of courageous surrender

Esther's declaration, "If I perish, I perish," stands among the bravest statements in Scripture. She did not deny the risk or pretend the danger was small. She faced it with open eyes and a surrendered heart. That same spirit defines the faithful life. Jesus said, "Whoever loses his life for my sake will find it" (Matt. 16:25). Courageous surrender means releasing control and trusting God with the outcome. For modern believers, it may not mean physical death, but it often requires sacrifice—perhaps reputation, comfort, or ambition. True discipleship costs something. Esther shows that surrender is not weakness; it is strength grounded in faith. When we entrust our lives fully to God's purpose, fear loses its grip, and obedience becomes our freedom. Courage begins where self-preservation ends.

4. Courage rooted in dependence

Before Esther acted, she called for fasting—a communal act of humility and dependence on God. Her courage did not spring from impulse or emotion but from prayerful surrender. Fasting implied seeking divine favor, aligning her will with God's. This balance between bold action and humble dependence is essential for Christians today. Courage without prayer becomes reckless; prayer without courage becomes passive. Esther's example teaches us that obedience requires both—faith that prays and faith that acts. When fear tempts us to rely on our own strength, we must remember that true courage is cultivated in communion with God. Prayer steadies trembling hands and anchors the heart before risk. Our boldness must flow from trust, not pride. Like Esther, we step forward after kneeling down, knowing our strength comes from the unseen God who hears.

5. The wisdom of patient faith

Twice Esther delayed revealing her request to the king, choosing to wait for the right moment. Her hesitation was not cowardice but discernment. Faithful obedience sometimes requires immediate action, but often it demands patient restraint. Esther's waiting allowed God's plan to ripen and the timing to align perfectly. In our lives, the same tension exists. We want results quickly, but God often works through waiting. Waiting refines faith, deepens trust, and reveals whether our confidence lies in his will or our own urgency. Patience is not passivity—it is faith stretched over time. Esther teaches that courage and wisdom walk hand in hand: courage to act when God says go, and wisdom to wait when he says not yet. The God who governs timing calls us to trust that his pace is perfect.

CONCLUSION

Esther 4:1–5:8 brings us to the turning point of the book. The decree of death has gone out, but in the ashes of mourning rises the courage of a queen. Mordecai's challenge reminded Esther that she was not in her position by chance, and Esther's resolve marked her transformation from silence to boldness. With fasting, prayer, and trust in God's providence, she stepped forward in faith, ready to risk her life for her people. God's purposes are certain, and he places his people where he wants them for reasons bigger than they can see. Our call is to be faithful when the moment comes.

REFLECTION

1. How did Mordecai and the Jews publicly respond to Haman's decree?
2. What was Esther's first reaction to Mordecai's call to approach the king?
3. What warning and assurance did Mordecai give Esther about remaining silent?
4. What did Esther ask the Jews to do before she approached the king?
5. How did Esther demonstrate courage when she went before the king?
6. Why did Esther delay her request and host two banquets instead?

DISCUSSION

1. When have you had to choose between silence and speaking up for truth?
2. How might God be using your current situation "for such a time as this"?
3. How can we better unite prayer and courage when making difficult decisions?
4. What does surrender to God's will look like in daily discipleship?
5. Why is waiting sometimes as important as courage in obeying God's will?
6. How does Esther's story help us trust God's providence when he seems silent?

5

PRIDE HUMBLED, FAITH EXALTED

ESTHER 5:9-6:14

Objective: To see how pride collapses under God's providence

INTRODUCTION

Have you ever watched two events unfold at the same time—one heading toward disaster, the other toward rescue—without either side knowing what the other was doing? It's like two trains speeding toward the same crossing: one carrying pride and destruction, the other bearing grace and deliverance. That's exactly what happens in this section of Esther.

The story takes a dramatic turn in these verses. Haman, fresh from dining with the king and queen, left the palace swollen with pride. But his joy evaporated when he saw Mordecai sitting at the gate, unmoved and unafraid. Pride that had been fed by honor was starved by defiance, and Haman resolved to destroy Mordecai once and for all. At his wife's urging, he ordered gallows built, confident that the next day would bring his triumph.

Yet while hammers rang in Haman's courtyard, the king could not sleep. In the middle of the night, he asked for the chronicles to be read and discovered that Mordecai's act of loyalty in saving his life had gone unrewarded. At the very moment Haman was plotting death, the king was preparing honor. Pride makes its plans, but providence writes the story.

These chapters remind us that God works in the smallest details, and his timing is always perfect.

EXAMINATION

Haman's pride and Mordecai's defiance (5:9-14)

When Esther left the first banquet, Haman was at the height of his pride. He had dined with the king and queen alone, an honor unmatched in the empire. He strutted out of the palace full of joy, his head swollen with self-importance. But as he passed the king's gate, there sat Mordecai. Once again, Mordecai refused to rise or show fear in his presence. The sight shattered Haman's mood. In an instant, joy curdled into rage. Pride had made him fragile, and Mordecai's quiet defiance was enough to undo him completely.

Haman restrained himself long enough to go home, where he gathered his friends and family. There he poured out both his boasting and his bitterness. He recounted his wealth, his sons, his promotions, and the special invitation to dine with the king and queen. Then came the complaint that spoiled it all: "But all this gives me no satisfaction as long as I see Mordecai the Jew sitting at the king's gate." For all his power and possessions, one man's refusal to bow stole his joy. That is the corrosive power of pride. It blinds us to blessings and chains us to bitterness over what we can't control.

Haman's wife Zeresh and his friends gave him the counsel his ego craved. They suggested he build a gallows fifty cubits high—a grotesquely oversized instrument of death—and ask the king in the morning to have Mordecai hanged upon it. Then, they told him, he could go merrily to the second banquet with the king and queen. The idea pleased Haman, and he ordered the gallows built. In his mind, the problem was as good as solved. Mordecai would be gone, his pride would be satisfied, and he would bask in royal favor unchallenged.

The sleepless king and the sovereign God (6:1-9)

But that very night, the king could not sleep. The timing was no accident. While Haman's servants hammered away at the gallows, God was at work in the sleeplessness of the king. Xerxes ordered the book of chronicles to be read to him, perhaps hoping the dry record of daily affairs would lull him back to sleep. Instead, the section read that night told of Mordecai's earlier act of loyalty in uncovering a plot against the king's life. The assassination attempt had been foiled because of Mordecai's vigilance. Yet when the king asked what had been done to honor him, the answer was, "Nothing."

The irony builds. Haman was preparing to ask for Mordecai's execution at the very moment the king was considering how to honor him. Pride plotted death while providence arranged recognition. The unseen hand of God turned sleeplessness, memory, and timing into the instruments of deliverance.

The next morning, as Haman entered the court eager to request Mordecai's death, the king was already looking for someone to advise him on how to honor this unknown man. When Haman arrived, the king asked, "What should be done for the man the king delights to honor?" Haman's pride leapt to conclusions. Who could the king possibly mean but him? Blinded by arrogance, Haman described in lavish detail the honor he craved: a royal robe the king had worn, a horse the king had ridden, a crown upon its head, and a noble official leading the honored man through the city proclaiming, "This is what is done for the man the king delights to honor!"

The great reversal (6:10–14)

The king listened, then gave the command Haman never expected: "Go at once. Get the robe and the horse, and do just as you have suggested for Mordecai the Jew, who sits at the king's gate. Do not neglect anything you have recommended." In one instant, Haman's dreams collapsed into humiliation. The man he sought to destroy was the one he was ordered to honor. And worse, he himself had to lead the parade.

Picture the scene: Haman, the second most powerful man in the empire, walking the streets of Susa with Mordecai astride the royal horse. His voice, once so full of boasting, now forced to proclaim words of honor he never meant. His humiliation was complete. Pride had plotted honor for itself but ended up exalting its enemy. Mordecai returned to the gate, unchanged and steady as always, while Haman rushed home in grief, his head covered in shame.

When he told his wife and friends what had happened, their response was chilling. They warned him that if Mordecai was of Jewish descent, Haman could not stand against him. They saw in this reversal the beginning of his downfall. Before he could even process their words, the king's eunuchs arrived to hurry him off to Esther's second banquet. The very gallows he had built for Mordecai now loomed as the symbol of his own impending fate.

This passage is rich with irony and reversal. Haman's pride built gallows for another, but God was preparing them for him. His arrogance dreamed of honor, but his humiliation became the stage for Mordecai's recognition. The king's sleepless night, an ordinary human inconvenience, became the hinge of history. What looked like coincidence was in fact providence.

The lesson is clear: pride brings ruin, while God's providence overturns the schemes of the wicked. Haman's downfall begins not in some dramatic battle but in his own living room, where bitterness festered, and in his own imagination, where pride blinded him. Mordecai's rise began not with self-promotion but with quiet faithfulness, an act of loyalty long forgotten by men but remembered by God at precisely the right moment.

Esther 5:9–6:14 reminds us that God's hand is never absent. He works through sleepless nights, remembered deeds, misjudged questions, and even the arrogance of the proud to bring about his purposes. For those who trust him, the message is one of profound hope. Evil may scheme, pride may rage, and injustice may seem to prevail, but the God who neither slumbers nor sleeps is always at work. His providence is never hurried, never delayed, and never thwarted. The gallows of the proud will not have the last word.

By the close of this section, the stage is set for Esther's decisive move. Mordecai had been honored, Haman had been humiliated, and the queen was prepared to reveal her petition. The tide was turning, not by human strength, but by the quiet orchestration of a God whose name is hidden in the text yet evident in every twist of the story.

APPLICATION

1. The poison of pride

This passage exposes pride as one of the most corrosive forces in the human heart. Haman had everything the world could offer—wealth, power, and position—yet he confessed that none of it satisfied him as long as Mordecai refused to bow. That is the tragedy of pride: it blinds us to blessings and enslaves us to bitterness. A single perceived insult becomes greater than all of God's goodness. Pride demands control, recognition, and praise, and when it fails to receive them, it breeds resentment. Left unchecked, it poisons relationships, distorts perspective, and devours joy. Again, scripture repeatedly warns that "pride goes before destruction" (Prov. 16:18), and Haman's story shows why. Pride destroys its host long before it harms anyone else. The call for Christians is to humble themselves before God, remembering that contentment, not control, is the mark of true spiritual strength.

2. The faithfulness of God's providence

While Haman plotted death, God was arranging deliverance. Mordecai's good deed, forgotten for years, resurfaced at the precise moment it mattered most. A sleepless king, a random page from the royal records, and an unexpected visitor converged into a perfect act of providence. None of it was coincidence. God never overlooks faithfulness, and nothing in our lives is wasted. Even what seems insignificant—a quiet act of service, a word of truth, a forgotten kindness—can become the hinge of history in God's timing. We often struggle to see how our small obedience fits into his grand design, but Esther reminds us that God is never late and never idle. When we trust his timing, we learn that what feels unnoticed is never unseen. His providence works silently but surely to exalt faithfulness and overturn evil.

3. The futility of opposing God's people

Haman's downfall began the moment he set himself against God's covenant people. His own wife and advisors recognized the truth he ignored: if Mordecai belonged to Israel, Haman could not stand. This reflects an eternal principle—no one can successfully oppose the purposes of God. Throughout history, the enemies of righteousness have risen and fallen, but God's people endure. Jesus assured his followers that the gates of hell will not prevail against his church (Matt. 16:18). The story of Haman illustrates that truth vividly. Evil may seem to prosper for a time, but its end is always defeat. For Christians, this is not a reason for arrogance but for confidence—not in ourselves, but in the faithfulness of God. When we suffer injustice or face opposition for our faith, we remember that God's covenant promises still stand, and his people remain secure.

4. The reward of humble faithfulness

The contrast between Mordecai and Haman could not be sharper. Haman craved honor and built gallows; Mordecai sought no recognition and waited quietly at the gate. Yet in the end, God exalted the humble and brought down the proud. This pattern echoes throughout Scripture: Joseph rose from prison, Daniel was vindicated after the lions' den, and Christ was glorified after the cross. True honor is never seized; it is given by God to those who serve him faithfully. The world urges us to chase success and recognition, but God calls us to quiet obedience. He sees the unseen and remembers what others overlook. Esther 5:9–6:14 reminds us that humility is not weakness but wisdom. Pride builds its gallows high, but faithfulness stands firm at the gate—and in God's time, the humble will be honored while the proud are brought low.

CONCLUSION

Esther 5:9–6:14 shows the rise and fall of pride in vivid detail. Haman's joy turned to rage at the sight of Mordecai, and his pride drove him to build gallows for his enemy. Yet in the same night, God worked through a sleepless king, a forgotten record, and a providential question to exalt Mordecai and humiliate Haman. The story reminds us that pride blinds and destroys, but God's providence overturns the schemes of the wicked. Even when his name is not mentioned, his hand directs every turn. For God's people, this passage is a call to humility, patience, and faith, trusting that the Lord will honor the faithful and bring down the proud.

REFLECTION

1. Why did Mordecai's refusal to bow anger Haman so deeply?
2. What plan did Haman's wife and friends suggest for Mordecai?
3. How did God use the king's sleepless night to alter events?
4. What did the king discover in the chronicles, and why was it important?
5. How did Haman misinterpret the king's question about honoring someone?
6. What were the outcomes for Mordecai and Haman in this passage?

DISCUSSION

1. How can pride steal our joy and peace like it did for Haman?
2. How can we guard against bitterness when others fail to recognize us?
3. How does God's perfect timing encourage us when our faithfulness feels unnoticed?
4. How have you seen pride lead to downfall in yourself or others?
5. How does this story build trust in God's providence through life's small "coincidences"?
6. How does God exalting the humble and humbling the proud challenge worldly values today?

6

TIME TO SPEAK

ESTHER 7

Objective: To trust God's providence and confront pride with courage and wisdom.

INTRODUCTION

Some moments in life feel like the pause before lightning strikes. The air is still, the sky heavy, and everyone senses that something decisive is about to happen. Then, in a flash, everything changes. That's the tension at the heart of Esther 7.

The book has been building toward this moment. For chapters we have watched tension rise—Mordecai's refusal to bow, Haman's rage, the decree of destruction, the gallows rising outside Haman's house, and the king's sleepless night that honored Mordecai instead of condemning him. Now the scene shifts to Esther's second banquet, where the queen will finally reveal her request.

Up to this point, Esther has walked a careful line of patience and timing. At her first banquet she spoke nothing of the plot. Instead, she waited, allowing Haman's pride to swell and the king's curiosity to deepen. Chapter 7 is the turning point. At last Esther breaks her silence, identifies herself with her people, and names Haman as the enemy. The mask is removed, and judgment falls.

This chapter reminds us that there comes a moment to speak, even at great cost. It reminds us that God humbles the proud and honors the faithful. And it reassures us that, even when his name is hidden, his providence directs every step toward justice and deliverance.

EXAMINATION

The moment of truth (7:1-6)

The chapter opens with the king and Haman attending Esther's second banquet. The first feast had raised the king's curiosity but offered no petition. Now, as they sat to drink wine, the king asked again what Esther desired, promising once more to grant it—even up to half the kingdom. The narrative slows here, as though to draw our attention to the suspense. Everything depends on Esther's words. For the first time in the book, she identifies herself with her people and pleads for their lives. She did not begin with accusations but with a plea: "Let my life be given me, and the life of my people."

Her words were carefully chosen. She did not denounce the decree in abstract terms but made it deeply personal. By tying her own fate to that of the Jews, she forced the king to see the matter not as distant politics but as a threat to his queen. She even explained that if her people had only been sold into slavery, she would have remained silent, but since they are sentenced to destruction, she could remain quiet no longer. The wisdom in her approach is striking. She honored the king, softened the ground with humility, yet presented the reality of the crisis with courage.

The king, perhaps startled by this sudden revelation, asked, "Who is he, and where is he, who has dared to do this?" The irony is sharp. The man sat right beside him. Esther spoke the words that shattered the room: "A foe and enemy—this wicked Haman." In a single sentence, the mask was ripped away, and the schemer was exposed.

The king's wrath and Haman's execution (7:7-10)

The king rose in wrath and stormed into the palace garden. His anger was real, but the text leaves us guessing what ran through his mind. Was he furious with Haman for endangering his queen, or angry at himself for being so easily manipulated? Perhaps both. Either way, he left the room in turmoil, and Haman realized his doom had arrived.

Desperation overtook him. No longer the proud official demanding honor, Haman now groveled before Esther, begging for his life. In his panic, he threw himself onto the couch where she reclined. At that precise moment, the king returned. Seeing Haman sprawled near his queen, Xerxes interpreted the scene as an assault. "Will he even violate the queen in my presence, in my own house?" the king cried. What began as a plea became the final nail in Haman's coffin.

The servants covered Haman's face, the symbol of his condemnation. One of the eunuchs, Harbona, spoke up, pointing out the gallows Haman had built for Mordecai, the very man who had saved the king's life. The irony is complete. The king ordered Haman to be hanged on it, and the chapter ends with a chilling reversal: the man who built gallows for another is executed on it himself.

This chapter is the literary and theological hinge of the book. Every detail drips with irony. The gallows meant for Mordecai became Haman's end. The queen who hid her identity now openly identified with her people. The enemy who sought to annihilate the Jews fell in disgrace. Pride was humbled, while the faithful were preserved.

But beyond the irony lies the clear providence of God. His name is still not mentioned, yet his fingerprints are everywhere. He orchestrated Esther's rise, Mordecai's forgotten loyalty, the sleepless night of the king, the perfect timing of the banquet, and the exposure of Haman's desperation. What the enemy planned for destruction, God turned to salvation.

Esther herself stands out in this chapter as a model of courage and wisdom. She could have raged at Haman or accused the king, but she chose her words with care. She honored Xerxes even as she revealed his folly, appealed to his self-interest even as she defended her people, and delivered her accusation at the precise moment it would have its greatest effect. Courage without wisdom might have failed; wisdom without courage would have remained silent. But together, courage and wisdom made her intercession effective.

Haman's downfall also serves as a sobering warning. The man who had risen so high in pride fell in a single day. His wealth, his sons, his honors, his access to the king—none could save him. He was destroyed by the very trap he had prepared for another. Scripture repeatedly tells us that God opposes the proud but gives grace to the humble (Prov. 3:34; Jas. 4:6; 1 Pet. 5:5). In Haman's end, we see that truth played out in unforgettable fashion.

Finally, we see the justice of God at work. Though the decree of destruction still loomed, the enemy has been struck down. God had begun to turn the tide. The salvation of his people would come in stages—first the exposure of the adversary, then the exaltation of his servants, and finally the deliverance of his nation. The pace of the story reminds us that God's justice often unfolds gradually, but it always unfolds surely.

By the end of Esther 7, the reader feels both relief and anticipation. Relief, because Haman is gone and the immediate threat has been removed. Anticipation, because the decree remains and the Jews are still in peril. The battle is not finished, but the decisive blow has been struck. The chapter stands as a monument to God's hidden providence, the courage of his servants, and the certainty that the proud will fall while the humble are lifted up.

APPLICATION

1. A time to speak

Esther 7 reminds us that there comes a moment when silence must end. For much of the story, Esther waited—listening, observing, and discerning the right time. But when the decisive hour arrived, she spoke with courage and conviction, identifying herself with her people. Her example challenges every believer to recognize when God calls us to step forward for truth and righteousness. Silence can feel safer, but obedience often demands risk. Speaking up for what is right may cost us comfort or security, yet faith requires action when God's purposes demand it. Esther's courage teaches us that the time to speak is not determined by fear or convenience but by conviction. When the moment comes, faith calls us to open our mouths, trust God's providence, and bear witness to his truth with boldness and grace.

2. Courage guided by wisdom

Esther's manner of speaking was as powerful as her message. She did not rage against injustice or accuse the king recklessly. Instead, she honored him, spoke with humility, and framed her plea with wisdom. Her courage was balanced by discernment—a reminder that truth must be spoken not only boldly but wisely. Boldness without wisdom can alienate; wisdom without boldness can fade into silence. God calls his people to embody both. We are to speak truth with grace, confront evil with humility, and pursue righteousness without arrogance. Esther shows that faithfulness is not loudness but precision—choosing words that pierce hearts rather than provoke hostility. In a world quick to shout and slow to listen, her example reminds us that courage and discernment are twin virtues. God's people must learn to speak both bravely and wisely for his glory.

3. The destructive end of pride

Haman's fall is a vivid warning of pride's fatal power. He built gallows for another but was executed on them himself. Pride always blinds before it destroys—it distorts perspective, feeds entitlement, and convinces us that our position makes us untouchable. Yet Scripture is clear: "Those who exalt themselves will be humbled" (Matt. 23:12). Pride separates us from others and ultimately from God. Haman's story calls us to self-examination, for pride can hide in the heart even when unspoken. It lurks behind defensiveness, comparison, and the hunger for control. God opposes the proud but gives grace to the humble. True greatness lies not in demanding honor but in submitting to the will of God. Haman's gallows stand as a solemn reminder: if we refuse humility, God will humble us; but if we bow low, he will lift us up.

4. The providence and justice of god

Though God's name never appears in Esther 7, his presence fills every line. The timing of the banquet, the king's wrath, Haman's panic, and Harbona's intervention all converge in perfect harmony. What seemed impossible for Esther was simple for the Lord. This chapter reassures believers that God's justice does not sleep. He can overturn the schemes of the wicked in an instant and vindicate his people in due time. For us, this is a source of deep comfort and confidence. We may face prideful powers, unjust systems, or seasons when God's hand seems hidden, yet he is always at work. The God who ruled the palace of Persia still rules today. Pride will fall, his people will stand, and his justice will prevail. Esther 7 reminds us that divine providence may be unseen, but it is never uncertain.

CONCLUSION

Esther 7 is the moment when everything hidden comes into the light. Esther finally spoke for her people, the king saw Haman's treachery, and the enemy was condemned to his own gallows. The chapter reminds us that silence must give way to courage, that words can be chosen with wisdom and still carry great boldness, and that pride always ends in ruin. Above all, it shows us the providence of God, who quietly arranges the timing, the setting, and the outcome. Though the decree against the Jews still stood, the adversary had been defeated. For us, the lesson is clear: God will honor the faithful, humble the proud, and bring justice in his perfect time.

REFLECTION

1. What request did Esther finally make during the second banquet?
2. How did Esther link her fate with that of her people?
3. What was the king's reaction to Esther's revelation of the threat?
4. How did Haman respond when his evil plan was exposed?
5. What misunderstanding led to Haman's final condemnation by the king?
6. How was Haman punished, and what irony marked his death?

DISCUSSION

1. How can we discern wise timing versus fearful silence when deciding to speak?
2. What does Esther's courage teach us about identifying with God's people today?
3. How can we speak truth with both courage and humility like Esther?
4. What subtle ways can pride appear in us, and how can we resist it?
5. How does God's providence here strengthen us against powerful opposition or impossible odds?
6. How does Esther 7 point to God's ultimate justice fulfilled through Christ?

7

JOY REMEMBERED IN PROVIDENCE

ESTHER 8-10

Objective: To celebrate God's providence and faithfulness that turns sorrow into joy.

INTRODUCTION

Have you ever watched a story that seemed hopeless until, in the final moments, everything turned around? A last-second goal, a long-awaited reunion, a plot twist that changes defeat into victory—such reversals stir something deep in us because they reflect the heart of God's story.

The story of Esther closes with a sweeping reversal. Though Haman had been executed in chapter 7, his decree of destruction remained. The Jews were still marked for death, and the empire's law could not be revoked. Yet what looked like an impossible situation became the stage for God's providence. The king gave Mordecai authority, and under his direction a new decree was written. Instead of being helpless victims, the Jews were empowered to stand and defend themselves.

The book ends with Mordecai exalted, the Jews secure, and God's providence on full display. Esther's story reminds us that even in exile, even under hostile decrees, God's promises stand, his people endure, and his providence turns mourning into celebration.

EXAMINATION

The crisis continues (8:1-17)

With Haman executed, one might expect the story to end. The villain is gone and justice has been served. But the danger had not disappeared. The decree of annihilation still hung over the Jews, sealed with the king's signet ring and spread across the empire. Persian law considered royal edicts irreversible, so though Haman was dead, his command lived on. The people of God were still scheduled for destruction on the thirteenth day of the twelfth month.

Esther 8 begins with a transfer of power. The king gave Haman's estate to Esther, who placed it under Mordecai's care. Mordecai was brought before the king, and Esther revealed their family connection. The king gave Mordecai his signet ring, the symbol of authority, the very ring once entrusted to Haman. The enemy's downfall became the servant's exaltation. The man who plotted death was disgraced, while the one he hated was clothed in royal robes of blue and white, crowned with gold, and honored throughout the city.

Yet Esther knew the crisis was not over. She fell at the king's feet, weeping and pleading for him to revoke Haman's edict. Once again she risked her life to intercede, though this time the king extended his scepter without hesitation. She begged him to find a way to save her people. Xerxes responded with a solution consistent with Persian law. He could not erase the first decree, but he could issue a new one to counter it. He instructed Esther and Mordecai to write in his name whatever they thought best, sealing it with the royal signet.

The counter-decree issued (8:7-14)

So the scribes were summoned, just as they had been when Haman dictated his deadly decree. But now the message was reversed. Instead of destruction, the Jews were authorized to assemble, defend themselves, and destroy anyone who attacked them. The decree was translated into every script and language, distributed across the empire, and hurried out by couriers on swift horses bred for the king's service. The scene mirrors chapter 3, but with a crucial difference: this time the news brought joy instead of confusion, hope instead of dread.

When the decree reached the provinces, the Jews celebrated with gladness and feasting. Many people of other nationalities, seeing the favor resting upon the Jews, declared themselves their allies. The empire that had once looked on them with suspicion now feared and respected them. The providence of God had turned despair into joy.

The day of reversal (9:1–32)

On the appointed thirteenth day of the twelfth month, when the enemies of the Jews had hoped to overpower them, the opposite happened. Because of the new decree, the Jews gathered to defend themselves. The officials of the provinces supported them, for fear of Mordecai had spread throughout the empire. The Jews struck down their enemies but did not lay hands on the plunder, showing that this was not about greed or gain but about survival and justice.

In Susa alone, five hundred men were killed, including the ten sons of Haman. Esther asked the king to permit their bodies to be displayed as a warning, and he agreed. The next day, three hundred more were struck down in the city. Across the provinces, seventy-five thousand enemies fell, but again, the Jews did not touch the plunder. Their restraint underscored that this was not vengeance or opportunism, but deliverance.

When the fighting ended, joy filled the land. What had begun as a day scheduled for their destruction became a day of victory and celebration. The Jews rested, feasted, and rejoiced, marking the day as one to be remembered for generations. From that time on, the festival of Purim was established. Named after the *pur* or lot that Haman had cast to decide the day of their destruction, the feast of Purim became a yearly reminder of God's providence, his reversal of fortune, and his deliverance of his people.

The book pauses here to describe how Purim was to be observed. It was not just a party, but a celebration of reversal—sorrow turned to joy, mourning turned to celebration. Families would exchange gifts of food and send provisions to the poor so that no one would be left out. Purim was a feast of memory, gratitude, and generosity. It ensured that the story of God's deliverance would never be forgotten, that future generations would remember how he preserved his people when destruction seemed certain.

Mordecai's exaltation and legacy (10:1–3)

These three verses close the book with a brief summary of Mordecai's greatness. He rose to second in rank after the king, honored among the Jews and respected throughout the empire. He sought the welfare of his people and spoke peace to them all. It is a fitting conclusion: the man who once sat quietly at the gate now stood as the protector of his people, exalted by the providence of God.

By the end of Esther, the laughter of chapter 1's banquets has been transformed. What began as the pride of a king and the schemes of a villain ends as the joy of God's people. The book closes with the unmistakable presence of the Lord's providence in the story. The hidden God had revealed his hand through reversals so dramatic they could not be chance. His people were saved, their enemies were defeated, and the memory of deliverance was etched forever in the feast of Purim.

APPLICATION

1. Providence redeems what it does not remove

The closing chapters of Esther remind us that God's providence does not always erase hardship, but it does redeem it. Even after Haman's execution, the decree of death remained. Deliverance came not by canceling the first decree but by empowering the Jews to defend themselves. God did not remove their danger—he gave them strength to stand in it. Likewise, faith does not promise an escape from every trial, but it assures us of God's sustaining grace through it. When hardship comes, the Christian's hope is not in comfort but in confidence that God equips his people for endurance. His providence may not always shield us from the storm, but it anchors us within it. Esther teaches us that deliverance sometimes comes not by the removal of trouble but by the renewal of courage, faith, and divine strength to face it.

2. The power and necessity of remembrance

Purim was more than a festival—it was an act of sacred memory. Each year, the Jews retold the story, shared food, and gave gifts to the poor so that everyone could rejoice together. Remembering kept their faith alive. Forgetfulness breeds fear and doubt, but remembrance strengthens trust.

Our faith also depends on memory: we remember God's deliverance through Scripture, worship, and especially the Lord's Supper, which proclaims Christ's victory until he comes again. When we recall God's faithfulness in the past, we find courage for the present. Forgetting what God has done leaves us vulnerable to despair, but remembrance rekindles gratitude and confidence. Esther's people looked back to a great reversal; Christians look back to an even greater one—the cross and the empty tomb. Memory transforms history into hope, reminding us that the God who saved yesterday is still at work today.

3. Joy that overflows in generosity

Purim was a feast marked not by selfish indulgence but by generosity. The joy of deliverance overflowed into giving—families shared food, exchanged gifts, and provided for the poor. Celebration became an expression of compassion. True gratitude always moves outward; when we recognize how richly God has blessed us, we naturally seek to bless others. Deliverance that stops at self-centered joy misses its purpose. God's grace is meant to flow through us, not terminate in us. The generosity of Purim points forward to Christian giving—the kind that springs from joy, not obligation. When our hearts overflow with thanksgiving, our hands open in kindness. The measure of gratitude is not how loudly we celebrate, but how freely we share. Esther's story calls us to mirror that spirit—to let every reminder of God's goodness lead us to generosity.

4. The faithfulness of God's covenant

Through every twist in Esther's story, one truth endures: God keeps his promises. He's the hero of this story. Though his people were scattered and threatened with extinction, his covenant faithfulness never wavered. The Jews were far from home, yet God preserved them just as he had promised Abraham—that his descendants would endure. The same faithfulness that sustained Esther's generation now anchors the church in Christ. No decree, empire, or adversary can erase what God has redeemed. He who preserved his people in Persia preserves his people still. In every age, believers stand secure because God's Word cannot fail. Esther's story proves that exile cannot erase divine purpose, and opposition cannot overturn divine promise. God's covenant love continues through Christ, in whom all his promises find their "yes" and "amen." When circumstances threaten faith, his unchanging faithfulness remains our anchor and our hope.

CONCLUSION

The final chapters of Esther bring the story full circle. What began with a decree of death ends with a festival of life. Haman's pride was shattered, Mordecai was exalted, and God's people were delivered. The feast of Purim became a lasting reminder that sorrow can turn to joy and mourning to celebration. God's providence is unmistakable, guiding every reversal. Esther's ending is both comfort and challenge—comfort, because God's promises never fail; challenge, because we are called to remember, to rejoice, and to live generously in response to his deliverance. The hidden God is faithful, and his people will endure.

REFLECTION

1. What authority did the king give Mordecai after Haman's execution?
2. Why could Haman's decree of destruction not simply be revoked?
3. What did the new decree allow the Jews to do on the appointed day?
4. How did the Jews respond when they heard the news of Mordecai's decree?
5. Why did the Jews refrain from taking plunder when they defeated their enemies?
6. What is the significance of the feast of Purim, and how was it to be celebrated?

DISCUSSION

1. How does God strengthen you when he doesn't remove struggles?
2. What helps you remember and celebrate God's faithfulness?
3. How can gratitude overflow into generosity toward others?
4. How does Mordecai's story reshape our view of success?
5. How can we trust God's unseen hand when he feels silent?
6. How does Esther's ending foreshadow Christ's greater reversal?

www.ingramcontent.com/pod-product-compliance
Lightning Source LLC
Chambersburg PA
CBHW052126070526
44586CB00016B/2099